LINES ON LUST

{a lover's bedside companion}

Compiled by Pamela Allardice

LOVE AND *lust* ALWAYS READ FROM THE SAME BOOK, BUT NOT ALWAYS FROM THE SAME PAGE.

Anonymous

Angus&Robertson

An imprint of HarperCollins*Publishers*

An Angus & Robertson Publication
Angus&Robertson, an imprint of HarperCollins Publishers
25 Ryde Road, Pymble, Sydney NSW 2073, Australia
31 View Road, Glenfield, Auckland 10, New Zealand
77 - 85 Fulham Palace Road, London W6 8JB, United Kingdom
10 East 53rd Street, New York NY 10022, USA

———•◆•———

First published in Australia in 1995
Compilation copyright © Pamela Allardice 1995

National Library of Australia
Cataloguing-in-Publication data
Lines on lust.
ISBN 0 207 18637 5.
1. Lust - Literary collections. I. Allardice, Pamela, 1958-.
808.803538
Printed in Hong Kong

Designed by X + Y Design

Photography by Anthony Adamson

9 8 7 6 5 4 3 2 1
98 97 96 95

THIS ANTHOLOGY OF POETRY AND PROSE CELEBRATES LUST IN ALL ITS MOODS AND GUISES. EXPRESSIONS OF LONGING, DESIRE AND SHEER ANIMAL PASSION SELECTED FROM *THE CANTERBURY TALES* AND THE *KAMA SUTRA*, THROUGH TO JOHN DONNE, ANDREW MARVELL, OMAR KHAYYÁM, D. H. LAWRENCE AND WILLIAM SHAKESPEARE ALL REVEAL THE ETERNAL NATURE OF FEELINGS OF LOVE AND LONGING. THIS COLLECTION REFLECTS ON THE VIOLENT SWINGS WE EXPERIENCE, FROM ECSTASY TO JEALOUSY AND THEN BACK TO PLAYFUL DELIGHT IN EACH OTHER'S COMPANY.

WITH POETRY, QUOTATIONS AND PLENTY OF 'JUICY BITS' FROM FAMOUS LOVERS, INCLUDING HENRY VIII'S LETTERS TO ANNE BOLEYN, WHAT ALEXANDRA WROTE IN HER DIARY ABOUT TSAR NICHOLAS, QUEEN VICTORIA'S DESCRIPTION OF HER WEDDING NIGHT WITH HER 'DEAR ALBERT', AND EVEN EXCERPTS FROM THE BIBLE, THIS COLLECTION BRINGS TOGETHER SOME OF THE BEST WRITING ON LUST, DESIRE AND LONGING OVER THE CENTURIES.

IT IS SURE TO BE A MUCH-CHERISHED — AND WELL-THUMBED — LITERARY BEDSIDE COMPANION!

I SLEEP, BUT MY HEART WAKETH: IT IS THE VOICE OF MY BELOVED THAT KNOCKETH, SAYING, OPEN TO ME, MY SISTER, MY LOVE, MY DOVE, MY UNDEFILED: FOR MY HEAD IS FILLED WITH DEW AND MY LOCKS WITH THE DROPS OF THE NIGHT.

I HAVE PUT OFF MY COAT; HOW SHALL I PUT IT ON? I HAVE WASHED MY FEET; HOW SHALL I DEFILE THEM?

MY BELOVED PUT IN HIS HAND BY THE HOLE OF THE DOOR, AND MY BOWELS WERE MOVED FOR HIM.

I ROSE UP TO *open* TO MY BELOVED; AND MY HANDS DROPPED WITH MYRRH, AND MY FINGERS WITH SWEET SMELLING MYRRH, UPON THE HANDLES OF THE LOCK.

I OPENED TO MY BELOVED; BUT MY BELOVED HAD WITHDRAWN HIMSELF, AND WAS GONE: MY SOUL FAILED WHEN HE SPAKE: I SOUGHT HIM, BUT I COULD NOT FIND HIM; I CALLED HIM, BUT HE GAVE ME NO ANSWER.

THE WATCHMEN THAT WENT ABOUT THE CITY FOUND ME, THEY SMOTE ME, THEY WOUNDED ME; THE KEEPERS OF THE WALLS TOOK AWAY MY VEIL FROM ME.

I CHARGE YOU, O DAUGHTERS OF JERUSALEM, IF YE FIND MY BELOVED, THAT YE TELL HIM, THAT I AM SICK OF LOVE.

from Song of Solomon, Chapter 5, verses 2 - 8

Sweet is the snow to heat-cracked lips,
Sweet the spring breeze to storm bound ships,
Sweetest of all when one cloak covers
On a summer night a pair of lovers.

John Bray, 'Comparisons', adapted from the Greek anthology

Love, my heart longs day and night for the meeting with you — for the meeting that is like all-devouring death.
Sweep me away like a storm; take everything I have; break open my sleep and *plunder* my dreams. Rob me of my world.
In that devastation, in the utter nakedness of spirit, let us become one in beauty.

from *The Gardener*, by Rabindranath Tagore

You are my *amazone mystique*. I believe in love through you, in you, with you. Without your love I want neither heaven nor earth ...
Let us love, my soul, my glorious amoreuse, in the sight of God and His Noble Son, Jesus Christ; and let no man separate those whom God has joined together for eternity.

from a letter from Franz Liszt to his mistress,
the Countess Marie d'Agoult

MY FIRST LOVE IS BUT FIFTEEN SPRINGS,
ALL HEAVEN'S IN HER EYES;
THE GIFT OF INNOCENCE SHE BRINGS,
WITH ME ALONE SHE LIES.
AND WHEN UPON MY KISS SHE CLINGS
SUCH RAPTURE DOES ARISE
MY LOINS BECOME TWO BEATING WINGS
THAT CLAMOUR AT HER THIGHS —
A SWAN THAT TOO INTENSELY SINGS
A DEATH-SONG ERE IT DIES.

Traditional, Chinese

How beautiful are thy feet with shoes, O prince's daughter! the joints of thy thighs are like jewels, the work of the hands of a cunning workman.

Thy navel is like a round goblet, which wanteth not liquor: thy belly is like an heap of wheat set about with lilies.

Thy two breasts are like two young roes that are twins.

Thy neck is as a tower of ivory; thine eyes like the fishpools in Heshbon, by the gate of Bath-rabbim: thy nose is as the tower of Lebanon which looketh towards Damascus.

Thine head upon thee is like Carmel, and the hair of thine head like purple; the king is held in the galleries.

How fair and how pleasant art thou, O love, for delights!

This thy stature is like to a palm tree, and thy breasts to clusters of grapes.

I said, I will go up to the palm tree, I will take hold of the boughs thereof: now also thy breasts shall be as clusters of the vine, and the smell of thy nose like apples;

And the roof of thy mouth like the best wine for my beloved, that goeth down sweetly, causing the lips of those that are asleep to speak.

I AM MY BELOVED'S, AND HIS *desire* IS TOWARD ME.

from Song of Solomon, Chapter 7, verses 1 - 10

AND THOU — WHAT NEEDST WITH THY TRIBES BLACK TENTS

WHO HAST THE RED PAVILION OF MY HEART?

Arab Love Song

———•◦•◦•———

WITH STUDY AS OUR PRETEXT, WE MADE OURSELVES WHOLLY FREE FOR LOVE, AND OUR LESSONS PROVIDED THE FURTIVE PRIVACY LOVE DESIRED; AND SO, THOUGH OUR BOOKS LAY OPEN, MORE WORDS OF LOVE PREVAILED THAN OF INSTRUCTION, MORE KISSES THAN PRECEPTS. HANDS MOVED MORE FREQUENTLY TO BREASTS THAN TO BOOKS. WHAT MORE CAN I SAY? IN OUR PASSION WE OMITTED NONE OF THE *steps* LOVERS TAKE, AND IF THERE WAS ANYTHING LESS USUAL OUR LOVE MIGHT DEVISE, THAT TOO WE ACCOMPLISHED. AND THE LESS VERSED WE HAD BEEN IN THOSE DELIGHTS, THE MORE ARDENTLY WE PURSUED THEM, AND THE LESS SATED WE BECAME.

✢ ✢ ✢

UNDER ALL THE CIRCUMSTANCES, GOD KNOWS, I HAVE FEARED OFFENDING YOU MORE THAN I HAVE FEARED OFFENDING HIM; AND IT IS YOU FAR MORE THAN GOD WHOM I WISH TO PLEASE. ONLY TELL ME, IF YOU CAN, WHY, SINCE THE RETIREMENT FROM THE WORLD WHICH YOU YOURSELF ENJOINED UPON ME, YOU HAVE NEGLECTED ME. TELL ME, I SAY, OR I WILL SAY WHAT I THINK, AND WHAT IS ON EVERYBODY'S LIPS. AH! IT WAS LUST RATHER THAN LOVE WHICH ATTRACTED YOU TO ME ...

Letters from Heloise to Abelard, c. 1098

SPRING IS EVEN NOW IN BLOSSOM;

WONDROUS IS THE WILLOW TREE

WHO SHALL WAKE THE UNKISSED DREAMER

TO A *tranquil ecstasy*

LONELY, LONELY HAVE I LANGUISHED; LONELY, LONELY HAVE I BEEN;

TELL ME, TELL ME, WILL IT VANISH,

NOW THAT I AM SEVENTEEN?

Traditional, Chinese

———

MY LOVE HUNG LIMP BENEATH THE LEAF

(O BITTER, BITTER SHAME!)

MY HEAVY HEART WAS FULL OF GRIEF

UNTIL MY LADY CAME.

SHE BROUGHT A TASTY DISH TO ME

(O SWOLLEN POD, AND SPRINGING SEED!)

MY LOVE SPRANG OUT RIGHT EAGERLY

TO SERVE ME IN MY NEED!

Elizabethan drinking song

———

DESIRES ARE NOURISHED BY DELAYS.

John Ray, *English Proverbs*

THEY ARE MOVED BY MAGIC

TO THE LOVER'S MOOD TO PASSION ..

spell

Virgil, *Eclogues*

These good fathers ... preach chastity to us, and want our wives. They dare not touch money ... but they are ready enough to handle women's thighs, which are far more dangerous.

Margaret of Navarre, *Novel VI*

Where desire doth bear the sway,
The heart must rule, the head obey.

Anonymous

He who loves without jealousy does not truly love.

The Zohar, 13th century

It is said that if a bunch of southernwood be laid under one's pillow, bed or bolster, it provoketh carnall copulation and resisteth all enchantments that hinder same.

from William Coles' *Herball*, 16th century

The anger of lovers renews their love.

Terence, *The Woman of Andros*, 166 B.C.

Mine own sweetheart, this shall be to advertise you of the great elengeness that I find here since your departing; for I ensure you methinketh the time longer since your departing now last than I was wont to do a whole fortnight. But now that I am coming towards you, methinketh my pains be half released, and I am wishing myself (specially an evening) in my sweetheart's arms, whose pretty dukkys I trust shortly to cusse. Written with the hand of him that was, is, and shall be yours by his will, H.R.

Henry VIII to Anne Boleyn, c. 1528

In the Spring, the river surges:
Fish of silver, fish of gold
Cast your *net* where fancy urges,
Gather all your nets will hold.
Once *net* fish is safely landed, damage not a single scale;
Only fools are heavy-handed
Only timid lovers fail.

Traditional, Chinese

It is the same in love as in war; a fortress that parleys is half taken.

Marguerite de Valois

THAT VERY TICKLING AND STING WHICH ARE IN CERTAIN PLEASURES, AND THAT SEEM TO RAISE US ABOVE SIMPLE HEALTH AND INSENSIBILITY: THAT ACTIVE, MOVING, AND, I KNOW NOT HOW, ITCHING AND BITING PLEASURE, EVEN THAT PLEASURE ITSELF AIMS AT NOTHING BUT INSENSIBILITY AS ITS MARK.

Montaigne, 'Apology for Raimond de Sebonde', *Essays*

MY LOVE IN HER ATTIRE DOTH SHEW HER WIT,
IT DOTH SO WELL *become* HER;
FOR EVERY SEASON SHE HATH DRESSINGS FIT,
FOR WINTER, SPRING AND SUMMER.
NO BEAUTY SHE DOTH MISS
WHEN ALL HER ROBES ARE ON:
BUT BEAUTY'S SELF SHE IS
WHEN ALL HER ROBES ARE GONE.

Anonymous

FEW ROMANTIC INTRIGUES CAN BE KEPT SECRET; MANY WOMEN ARE AS WELL KNOWN BY THE NAMES OF THEIR LOVERS AS THEY ARE BY THOSE OF THEIR HUSBANDS.

La Bruyere, 'Of Women', *Characters*, 1688

THE BLOOD OF YOUTH BURNS NOT WITH SUCH EXCESS

AS GRAVITY'S REVOLT TO WANTONNESS.

William Shakespeare, *Love's Labour's Lost*

FOR GLANCES BEGET OGLES, OGLES SIGHS,

SIGHS WISHES, WISHES WORDS, AND WORDS A LETTER, ...

AND THEN, GOD KNOWS WHAT MISCHIEF MAY ARISE,

WHEN LOVE LINKS TWO YOUNG PEOPLE IN ONE FETTER,

VILE ASSIGNATIONS, AND ADULTEROUS BEDS,

ELOPEMENTS, BROKEN VOWS AND HEARTS AND HEADS.

Lord Byron, *Beppo*

LUST IS A CONFLICT BETWEEN REFLEXES AND REFLECTIONS.

Anonymous

O WESTERN WIND, WHEN WILT THOU BLOW

THAT THE SMALL RAIN DOWN CAN RAIN?

CHRIST, IF MY LOVE WERE IN MY ARMS

AND I IN MY BED AGAIN!

Unknown 16th century poet

"HOW OFTEN WHEN THE RAGE AND TUMULT OF MY SENSES HAD SUBSIDED AFTER THE *melting* FLOW, HAVE I, IN A TENDER MEDITATION, ASK'D MYSELF COOLLY THE QUESTION, IF IT WAS IN NATURE FOR ANY OF ITS CREATURES TO BE SO HAPPY AS I WAS? OR, WHAT WERE THE FEARS OF THE CONSEQUENCE, PUT IN THE SCALE OF ONE NIGHT'S ENJOYMENT OF A THING SO TRANSCENDENTLY THE TASTE OF MY EYES AND HEART, AS THAT DELICIOUS, FOND AND MATCHLESS ... ?"

John Cleland, *The Memoirs of Fanny Hill,* **18th century**

FOR MEN HAVE EVER A LIKEROUS APPETITE

ON LOWER THINGS TO PERFORM THEIR DELIGHT

THAN ON THEIR WIVES, BE THEY NEVER SO FAIR.

NOR NEVER SO TRUE, NOR SO DEBONAIR.

FLESH IS NO NEWFANGEL, WITH MISCHAUNCE,

THAT WE CAN IN NO THING HAVE PLEASAUNCE

THAT TENDETH UNTO VIRTUE ANY WHILE.

Geoffrey Chaucer, *The Maunciple's Tale*, c. 1380

—•••—

A SWEET DISORDER IN THE DRESS

KINDLES IN CLOTHES A WANTONNESS

A LAWN ABOUT THE SHOULDERS THROWN

INTO A FINE DISTRACTION ...

A *careless* SHOESTRING IN WHOSE TIE

I SEE A WILD CIVILITY

DOES MORE BEWITCH ME, THAN WHEN ART

IS TOO PRECISE IN EVERY PART.

Robert Herrick

—•••—

LOVE IS A KIND OF WARFARE.

Ovid, *Ars Amatoria*, c. 1st century B.C.

AH LOVE! COULD YOU AND I WITH HIM CONSPIRE

TO GRASP THIS SORRY SCHEME OF THINGS ENTIRE,

WOULD NOT WE SHATTER IT TO BITS — AND THEN

RE-MOULD IT NEARER TO THE HEART'S DESIRE!

from *The Rubáiyát* of Omar Khayyám

THE DARTS OF LUST ARE IN THY EYES; AND THEREFORE FIX NOT THY EYE ON
THAT WHICH THOU MAYEST NOT DESIRE.

Margaret of Navarre, *Memoratives*

DO NOT GO, MY LOVE, WITHOUT ASKING MY LEAVE.

I HAVE WATCHED ALL NIGHT, AND NOW MY EYES ARE HEAVY WITH SLEEP.

I FEAR LEST I LOSE YOU WHEN I AM SLEEPING.

DO NOT GO, MY LOVE, WITHOUT ASKING MY LEAVE.

I START UP AND STRETCH MY HANDS TO TOUCH YOU. I ASK MYSELF, "IS IT A
DREAM?"

COULD I BUT *entangle* YOUR FEET WITH
MY HEART AND HOLD THEM FAST TO MY BREAST!

DO NOT GO, MY LOVE, WITHOUT ASKING MY LEAVE.

from *The Gardener*, by Rabindranath Tagore

WE MUST NOT RIDICULE A PASSION WHICH HE WHO NEVER FELT NEVER WAS
HAPPY, AND HE WHO LAUGHS AT NEVER DESERVES TO FEEL.

Dr Johnson

BEING YOUR SLAVE, WHAT SHOULD I DO BUT TEND
UPON THE HOURS AND TIMES OF YOUR DESIRE?
I HAVE NO PRECIOUS TIME AT ALL TO SPEND,
NOR SERVICES TO DO, TILL YOU REQUIRE.

NOR DARE I CHIDE THE WORLD-WITHOUT-END HOUR
WHILST I, MY SOVEREIGN, WATCH THE CLOCK FOR YOU,
NOR THINK THE BITTERNESS OF ABSENCE SOUR
WHEN YOU HAVE BID YOUR *servant* ONCE ADIEU;

NOR DARE I QUESTION WITH MY JEALOUS THOUGHT
WHERE YOU MAY BE, OR YOUR AFFAIRS SUPPOSE,
BUT LIKE A SAD SLAVE, STAY AND THINK OF NOUGHT
SAVE, WHERE YOU ARE, HOW HAPPY YOU MAKE THOSE.

SO TRUE A FOOL IS LOVE, THAT IN YOUR WILL
THOUGH YOU DO ANYTHING, HE THINKS NO ILL.

William Shakespeare, 'Absence'

I stole a look at him, and met his Gypsy eyes — those eyes which looked through you, glazed over, and saw something behind; the only man I have ever seen, not a Gypsy, with that peculiarity ...

[I] grew red and pale, hot and cold, dizzy and faint ...

One day an exception was made to our dull rule of life. My cousin gave a tea-party and dance and the great majority flocked in, and there was Richard like a star among the rushlights! That was a night of nights; he waltzed with me once, and spoke to me several times, and I kept my sash where he put his arm round my waist to waltz, and my gloves, which his hands had clasped. I never wore them again. Shall I never be at rest with him to love and understand me, to tell every thought and feeling in far different scenes from here? Under canvas in Rangoon ...

If Richard and I never marry, God will cause us to meet in the next world; we cannot be parted, we belong to each other. A dry crust, privations, pain, danger for him I love ... There is something in some women that seems born for the knapsack. There is only one man in the world who could be master of such a spirit as mine. People may love (as it is called) a thousand times, but the real *feu sacré* only burns once in one's life ...

Isabel Arundell,
on her first meeting with Sir Richard Burton

For everything created
In the bounds of earth and sky,
Hath such longing to be mated,
It must *couple* or must die.

Anonymous

In the morning she rose disarrayed, and her eyes betrayed a night without slumber; when the yellow-robed God, who gazed on her with transport, thus meditated on her charms in his heavenly mind: "Though her locks be diffused at random, though the lustre of her lips be faded, though her garland and zone be hidden from their enchanting stations, and though she hide the places with her hands, looking towards me in bashful silence, yet even thus disarranged she fills me with extatick delight".

The Hindu god Krishna, describing his lover Radha, from Jayadeva's *Gita Govinda*

Love comforteth like sunshine after rain,
But Lust's effect is tempest after sun;
Love's gentle spring doth always fresh remain,
Lust's winter comes ere summer half be done:
Love surfeits not. Lust like a glutton dies;
Love is all truth, Lust full of forged lies.

William Shakespeare, *Venus and Adonis*

Passion is universal humanity. Without it romance would be useless.

Balzac

I DO NOT LOVE THEE! —

No!

I DO NOT LOVE THEE!

And yet when thou art absent I am sad;
And envy even the bright blue sky above thee,
Whose quiet stars may see thee and be glad.

I do not love thee! — yet, I know not why,
Whate'er thou dost seems still well done, to me:
And often in my solitude I sigh
That those I do love are not more like thee!

I do not love thee! — yet, when thou art gone,
I hate the sound (though those who speak be dear)
Which breaks the lingering echo of the tone
Thy voice of music leaves upon my ear.

I do not love thee! — yet thy speaking eyes,
With their deep, bright, and most expressive blue,
Between me and the midnight heaven arise,
Oftener than any other eyes I ever knew.

I know I do not love thee! yet, alas!
Others will scarcely trust my candid heart;
And oft I catch them smiling as they pass,
Because they see me gazing where thou art.

Carolina Elizabeth Sarah Norton, c. 1820

THE PLEASURE OF LOVE IS LOVING, AND WE GET MORE HAPPINESS FROM THE PASSION WE FEEL THAN FROM THE PASSION WE INSPIRE.

La Rochefoucauld, *Maxims*, 1655

———•••———

WE HAVE JOYS QUITE UNLIKE THOSE OF OTHERS ... FEW HAVE A LIFE LIKE OURS. HOW WE LOVE TO LOVE! ... HE SAYS HE KNOWS ONLY ONE THING ... SINCE THE WORLD BEGAN, NO MAN OF HIS AGE HAS EVER LOVED A WOMAN AS HE LOVES ME ... I STAY WITH HIM WHILE HE WRITES THE WORDS [OF *SIEGFRIED*] ... MY CUP OVERFLOWS WITH *rapture* IN OUR HOUSE OF HAPPINESS.

Cosima von Bulow, writing of her love for Richard Wagner, 1870

———•••———

(MY) AURORA'S EYES ARE VEILED, THEY ONLY SHINE WHEN I PLAY: THEN THE WORLD IS LIGHT AND LOVELY. MY FINGERS GLIDE SOFTLY OVER THE KEYS, HER PEN FLIES OVER THE PAPER. SHE LIKES TO WRITE TO MUSIC. MUSIC ALL AROUND HER — CHOPIN'S MUSIC, SOFT BUT CLEAR, LIKE WORDS OF LOVE. FOR YOU, AURORE, I WILL PLAY MY SWEETEST MELODIES. MY DARLING, WITH YOUR VEILED EYES — YOU WON'T BE TOO CRUEL, WILL YOU?

Frederic Chopin, writing in his journal of his lover,

George Sand, c. 1850

WOMAN IS LIKE A FRUIT, WHICH WILL NOT YIELD ITS SWEETNESS UNTIL YOU *rub it* BETWEEN YOUR HANDS. LOOK AT THE BASIL PLANT; IF YOU DO NOT

rub it WARM WITH YOUR FINGERS IT WILL NOT EMIT ANY SCENT. DO YOU NOT KNOW THAT THE AMBER, UNLESS IT BE HANDLED AND WARMED, KEEPS HIDDEN WITHIN ITS PORES THE AROMA CONTAINED IN IT. IT IS THE SAME WITH WOMAN. IF YOU DO NOT ANIMATE HER WITH YOUR TOYING, INTERMIXED WITH KISSING, NIBBLING AND TOUCHING, YOU WILL NOT OBTAIN FROM HER WHAT YOU ARE WISHING; YOU WILL FEEL NOT ENJOYMENT WHEN YOU SHARE HER COUCH, AND YOU WILL WAKEN IN HER HEART NEITHER INCLINATION NOR AFFECTION, NOR LOVE FOR YOU; ALL HER QUALITIES WILL REMAIN HIDDEN...

IF YOU SEE A WOMAN HEAVING DEEP SIGHS, WITH HER LIPS GETTING RED AND HER EYES LANGUISHING, WHEN HER MOUTH HALF OPENS AND HER MOVEMENTS GROW HEEDLESS; WHEN SHE APPEARS TO BE DISPOSED TO GO TO SLEEP, VACILLATING IN HER STEPS AND PRONE TO YAWN, KNOW THAT THIS IS THE MOMENT FOR COITION; AND IF YOU THERE AND THEN MAKE YOUR WAY INTO HER YOU WILL PROCURE FOR HER AN UNQUESTIONABLE TREAT. YOU YOURSELF WILL FIND THE MOUTH OF HER WOMB CLASPING YOUR ARTICLE, WHICH IS UNDOUBTEDLY THE CROWNING PLEASURE FOR BOTH, FOR THIS BEFORE EVERYTHING BEGETS AFFECTION AND LOVE...

THE KISS IS ASSUMED TO BE AN INTEGRAL PART OF COITION. THE BEST KISS IS THE ONE IMPRESSED ON HUMID LIPS COMBINED WITH THE SUCTION OF THE LIPS AND TONGUE, WHICH LATTER PARTICULARLY PROVOKES THE FLOW OF SWEET AND FRESH SALIVA. IT IS FOR THE MAN TO BRING THIS ABOUT BY SLIGHTLY AND SOFTLY

NIBBLING HIS PARTNER'S TONGUE, WHEN HER SALIVA WILL FLOW SWEET AND
EXQUISITE, MORE PLEASANT THAN REFINED HONEY ... THIS MANOEVRE WILL GIVE
THE MAN A TREMBLING SENSATION, WHICH WILL RUN ALL THROUGH HIS BODY,
AND IS MORE INTOXICATING THAN WINE DRUNK TO EXCESS.

from *The Perfumed Garden of the Shaykh Nefzawi*, c. 1876

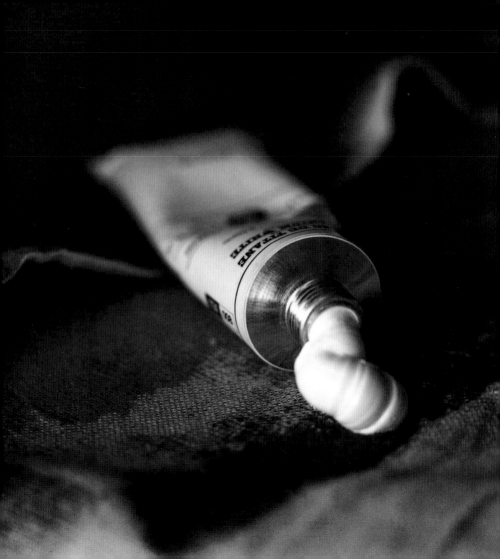

I don't think I can properly wait [for your return] until my picture is done. My hands tremble so I can scarcely write, and my head is swimming. It would be much better if I didn't tell you all this but I am past all control. Tell me when I might come, and I would come with the small picture and paint there. It would not be fair to keep us [apart] till July past [sic.] You musn't be upset. I only tell you what should be a sense of congratulation to yourself that you are so much in my thoughts. I can draw occasionally, but I know I couldn't paint a bit ... As the chance approaches of seeing and living with you I grow *more impatient.* I am really a good husband, though I says what shouldn't, for I am very unfitted for such a lengthened separation as I have had to bear. We shall be the happier I am sure when we do meet. Now you understand clearly ... It is quite impossible for me to do this all alone as Nature won't stand it. If you could join me in a few days here I would work twice as fast and have no irritation.

John Everett Millais, to his wife, Euphemia, 1865

—◦•◦—

To be with those one loves is enough: to dream, to talk with them, or to remain silent — one with them: thinking of them or thinking of nothing in particular, but beside them — then all is well.

La Bruyère

"IS IT DAY?" SHE SAID, LAYING HER HEAD ON HIS BREAST, SUDDENLY.

"AY! IT'S ABOUT FIVE."

SHE HEARD THE RESONANCE OF HIS VOICE, AND OPENED HIS SHIRT, TO LAY HER
EAR OVER HIS HEART. THUD! THUD! SO DEEP! SHE SOFTLY KISSED THE MAN'S
BREAST-NIPPLE. HE HAD DRAWN HER CLOSE AND WITH INFINITE DELICATE
PLEASURE WAS STROKING THE FULL, SOFT,

vOluptuOus

CURVE OF HER LOINS. SHE DID NOT KNOW WHICH WAS HIS HAND AND WHICH
WAS HER BODY, IT WAS LIKE A FULL BRIGHT FLAME, SHEER LOVELINESS.
EVERYTHING IN HER FUSED DOWN IN PASSION, NOTHING BUT THAT ...

SHE LAUGHED TO HERSELF AFTER A WHILE, FEELING HIS WEIGHT MOTIONLESS
UPON HER. SHE LOVED IT SO. AND SHE THOUGHT: "AND THE GRASSHOPPER
SHALL BE A BURDEN AND DESIRE SHALL FAIL —" WAS IT FROM THE BIBLE? HOW
AWFUL IF DESIRE SHOULD FAIL! HOW GRATEFULLY SHE LOVED HIM, THAT HIS
DESIRE DID NOT FAIL.

from *The First Lady Chatterley*, by D. H. Lawrence, 1944

———•••———

A PASSIONATE NATURE ALWAYS LOVES WOMEN, BUT ONE WHO LOVES
WOMEN IS NOT NECESSARILY A PASSIONATE NATURE.

Chang Ch'ao, *Sweet Dream Shadows*, mid 17th century

FIDELINA, MY ONE AND ONLY BELOVED:

I WILL BORE YOU ONCE AGAIN WITH MY THOUGHTS ON THE SUBJECT OF INSPIRATION AND CREATIVITY, BUT AS YOU WILL PERCEIVE THESE THOUGHTS ARE DIRECTLY CONNECTED WITH YOU...

TO ME YOU ARE THE GATE OF *Paradise.* FOR YOU I WILL RENOUNCE FAME, CREATIVITY, EVERYTHING. FIDELINE, FIDELINA — I LONG FOR YOU INTENSELY AND FRIGHTFULLY.

I'M SHIVERING AS IF ANTS WERE RUNNING UP MY SPINE TO MY HEAD. WHEN YOU FINALLY ARRIVE IN YOUR DILIGENCE I WILL GLUE MYSELF TO YOU, SO THAT FOR A WHOLE WEEK YOU WONT [SIC] BE ABLE TO TEAR ME AWAY FROM THE LITTLE D FLAT MAJOR, AND TO HELL WITH INSPIRATION AND IDEAS. LET MY COMPOSITION DISAPPEAR IN THE DARK FOREVER...

HOFFMAN JUST CAME AND SCATTERED TO THE WIND THE POSSIBILITY OF WRITING A LETTER. THE PUPILS WILL SHORTLY ARRIVE AS WELL, I WILL THEREFORE FINISH, SO THAT MY LETTER CAN LEAVE BY TODAY'S MAIL. I KISS YOUR BELOVED LITTLE BODY ALL OVER.

YOUR MOST FAITHFUL FREDERIC
YOUR ENTIRELY FAITHFUL FREDERIC
YOUR *MOST* GIFTED PUPIL, ONE WHO HAS SKILFULLY MASTERED THE ART OF MAKING LOVE.

Frederic Chopin to Delphine Potocka

HE CAN TALK OF NOTHING BUT KISSES — KISSES EVERYWHERE — AND UPON
PORTIONS OF THE ANATOMY NOT TO BE FOUND IN ANY DICTIONARY OF THE
ACADEMIE FRANÇAISE ...

M. Mérimée, on collecting and editing
Napoleon Bonaparte's letters, c. 1806

PARIS, DECEMBER 1795

I WAKE FILLED WITH THOUGHTS OF YOU. YOUR PORTRAIT AND THE INTOXICATING
EVENING WHICH WE SPENT YESTERDAY HAVE LEFT MY SENSES IN TURMOIL.
SWEET, INCOMPARABLE JOSEPHINE, WHAT A STRANGE EFFECT YOU HAVE ON MY
HEART! ARE YOU ANGRY? DO I SEE YOU LOOKING SAD? ARE YOU WORRIED? ...
MY SOUL ACHES WITH SORROW, AND THERE CAN BE NO REST FOR YOUR LOVER;
BUT IS THERE STILL MORE IN STORE FOR ME WHEN, YIELDING TO THE PROFOUND
FEELINGS WHICH OVERWHELM ME, I DRAW FROM YOUR LIPS, FROM YOUR HEART
A LOVE WHICH *consumes* ME WITH FIRE? AH! IT WAS LAST NIGHT THAT I FULLY
REALISED HOW FALSE AN IMAGE OF YOU YOUR PORTRAIT GIVES!

YOU ARE LEAVING AT NOON; I SHALL SEE YOU IN THREE HOURS.

UNTIL THEN, MIO DOLCE AMOR, A THOUSAND KISSES; BUT GIVE ME NONE IN
RETURN, FOR THEY SET MY BLOOD ON FIRE.

A letter from Napoleon Bonaparte to Josephine Beauharnais

LUST'S AN HONEST ROBBER,
BLUDGEONING FOR SEX.
LOVE'S A WHINING CON-MAN,
PASSING PHONEY CHEQUES.

LUST IS INTERMITTENT,
SUPS HIS FILL AND SLEEPS.
LOVE FROM DAWN TO SUNRISE
CASTIGATES OR CREEPS.

LUST IS *standard issue* —
MEN OR PIGS OR GEESE.
LOVE'S A VISITATION
FROM SOME GOD'S CAPRICE.

LUST CAN BE DIVERTED
TOWARDS ANOTHER GOAL
LOVE IS MONOMANIC
COMPASS TO THE POLE.

YET SOME SAY THE PRIZE PIECE
LIFE'S MINT EVER COINED
COMES WHEN BY SOME CHANCE FREAK
LUST AND LOVE ARE JOINED.

John Bray, 'Lust and Love'

BLUE EYES SAY, 'LOVE ME OR I DIE'; BLACK EYES SAY, 'LOVE ME OR I KILL THEE.'

Spanish proverb

SHE LOOKED VERY BEAUTIFULL WITH SOME RED ROSES IN HER HAT AND THE DAINTY RED RUGE IN HER CHEEKS LOOKED QUITE THE THING. BERNARD HEAVED A SIGH AND HIS EYES FLASHED AS HE BEHELD HER AND ETHEL THORGHT TO HERSELF WHAT A FINE TYPE OF MANHOOD HE REPRISENTED ... BERNARD SAT BESIDE HER IN PROFOUND SILENCE GAZING AT HER PINK FACE AND LONG WAVY EYE LASHES ...

ETHEL HE MURMURED IN A TREMBLY VOICE.

OH WHAT IS IT SAID ETHEL HASTILY SITTING UP.

WORDS FAIL ME EJACULATED BERNARD HORSLY MY PASSION FOR YOU IS INTENSE HE ADDED *fervently*. IT HAS GROWN DAY AND NIGHT SINCE I FIRST BEHELD YOU.

OH SAID ETHEL IN SUPPRISE I AM NOT PREPARED FOR THIS AND SHE LENT BACK AGAINST THE TRUNK OF THE TREE.

BERNARD PLACED ONE ARM TIGHTLY AROUND HER. WHEN WILL YOU MARRY ME ETHEL HE UTTERED YOU MUST BE MY WIFE IT HAS COME TO THAT I LOVE YOU SO INTENSLY THAT IF YOU SAY NO I SHALL PERFORCE DASH MY BODY TO THE BRINK OF YON MUDDY RIVER HE PANTED WIDLY.

OH DON'T DO THAT IMPLORED ETHEL BREATHING RARTHER HARD.

THEN SAY YOU LOVE ME HE CRIED.

OH BERNARD SHE SIGHED FERVENTLY I CERTAINLY LOVE YOU MADLY YOU ARE TO ME LIKE A HEATHEN GOD SHE CRIED LOOKING AT HIS MANLY FORM AND HANDSOME FLASHING FACE I WILL INDEED MARRY YOU.

A Proposal, from *The Young Visiters*, by Daisy Ashford

... HE WAS SO DEAR AND KIND. WE HAD OUR DINNER IN OUR SITTING ROOM, BUT I HAD SUCH A SICK HEADACHE THAT I COULD EAT NOTHING, AND WAS OBLIGED TO LIE DOWN ... FOR THE REMAINDER OF THE EVENING ON THE SOFA; BUT ILL OR NOT, I NEVER, NEVER SPENT SUCH AN EVENING!! MY DEAREST, DEAREST ALBERT SAT ON A FOOTSTOOL BY MY SIDE, AND HIS EXCESSIVE LOVE AND AFFECTION GAVE ME FEELINGS OF HEAVENLY LOVE AND HAPPINESS I NEVER COULD HAVE HOPED TO HAVE FELT BEFORE! HE CLASPED ME IN HIS ARMS, AND WE KISSED EACH OTHER AGAIN AND AGAIN! HIS BEAUTY, HIS SWEETNESS AND GENTLENESS – REALLY HOW CAN I EVER BE THANKFUL ENOUGH TO HAVE SUCH A HUSBAND! ... TO BE CALLED BY NAMES OF TENDERNESS, I HAVE NEVER YET HEARD USED TO ME BEFORE – WAS BLISS BEYOND BELIEF! OH! THIS WAS THE HAPPIEST DAY OF MY LIFE! – MAY GOD HELP ME TO DO MY DUTY AS I OUGHT AND BE WORTHY OF SUCH BLESSINGS!

from Queen Victoria's diary, on her honeymoon

A LITTLE SHE STROVE, AND MUCH REPENTED
AND WHISPERING 'I'LL NE'ER CONSENT' – *consented*

Lord Byron, *Don Juan*

THE RULING PASSION, BE WHAT IT WILL,
THE RULING PASSION CONQUERS REASON STILL.

Alexander Pope, *Moral Essays*

AND AS CHOCOLATE PROVOKES OTHER EVACUATIONS THROUGH THE FEVERAL EMUNCTORIES OF THE BODY, SO IT DOTH THAT OF SEED, AND BECOMES PROVOCATIVE TO LUST UPON NO OTHER ACCOUNT ...

Henry Stubbs, c. 1650

THE SEA HATH BOUNDS, BUT DEEP DESIRE HATH NONE.

William Shakespeare, *Venus and Adonis*

WHAT MEN CALL GALLANTRY, AND GODS ADULTERY,
IS MUCH MORE COMMON WHERE THE CLIMATE'S SULTRY.

Lord Byron, *Don Juan*

CHRISTIANITY HAS DONE A GREAT DEAL FOR LOVE BY
MAKING A  OF IT.

Anatole France, *The Garden of Epicurus,* **1894**

IT IS IN THE HALF-LIGHT OF THE BEDOUIN ARAB TENT THAT ONE MUST SEEK THE MODEL OF TRUE LOVE.

Stendhal

AFTER A NIGHT SOARING THROUGH TARZAN'S SHEETS,
THIS WAS MY *routine*:

> 1. HEAD HOME
> 2. MAINLINE CAFFEINE
> 3. FLIP THROUGH MAIL
> 4. CHECK FOR PIMPLES; DID HE NOTICE?

BY THE TIME I BRUSHED MY TEETH
I HAD GONE OVER WHETHER
I SHOULD HAVE DONE WHAT I DID WITH WHOMEVER.
THEN I WAS OFF AGAIN,
TOO RUSHED FOR A SHOWER.

PEOPLE I'D JOSTLE IN BUSES WOULD LOOK A BIT QUEER;
THE BLIND NEWSMAN KNEW,
HE HAD NOSTRILS QUICK AS A SPANIEL'S.
BUT THAT WAS LIFE BEFORE LUXURIOUS YOU.

NOW WE SHOWER EACH MORNING,
THE SPRAY STICKY-FINGERED AS THE BED
WE CAN'T GET OUT OF,
WE'RE SWIMMING IN EACH OTHER,
WE MELT LIKE CANDLES THAT HAVE BURNT OUT
AS WE SCENTED DOWN EVERY TRAIL OF OUR BODIES,
SNUFFLING IN CULVERTS, IN VALLEYS, ROLLING IN THE STREAM
WITH OUR LEGS IN THE AIR.

MY FINGERPRINTS CARRY YOUR FACE.
I FIND GOLD IN MY HAIR.
YOUR RIBS ARE TATTOOED ON MINE.

I DON'T NEED YOUR SCENT RISING LIKE JUNGLE MIST,
YOU RUN THROUGH MY VEINS,
A SECRET DEPOSIT I CAN MINE
AND NO ONE ELSE KNOWS.
YOU GLITTER INSIDE, YOU TRAP LIGHT,
YOU'RE WORTH MORE THAN COUNTERS THAT TICK TO YOUR HEAT,
YOU SMOULDER, WE'LL EXPLODE TONIGHT:
VOLCANIC RIVERS RUNNING DOWN TO THE SEA.

Jeri Kroll, 'Showers'

YOU'RE THE OBSTINATE HARDY GRASS

WHICH KEEPS ON GROWING BACK

THROUGH THE FLOORBOARDS

OF MY MIND

AFTER ALL MY ATTEMPTS

AT PRUNING, AT *Rationalisation*

YOU STUBBORNLY ENDURE

DEMANDING: TAKE THIS AS IT IS.

DARLING, IN THE INNER

COURTYARD OF MY HEART

YOU SLEEP AND TURN BESIDE ME

LIKE A SHIP CHANGING COURSE

MID-DREAM; SOMEWHERE

IN THAT PRIVATE TERRITORY

WHICH LIES BEHIND CLOSED EYES.

Irene Wettenhall, 'Inner Courtyard of the Heart'

THERE IS NOTHING LIKE DESIRE

FOR PREVENTING THE THING ONE SAYS

FROM BEARING ANY RESEMBLANCE TO WHAT ONE HAS IN ONE'S MIND.

Marcel Proust, *Remembrance of Things Past*

I HAD MET HER, PRIMARILY, IN THE STREET. YOU KNOW HOW THE THING HAPPENS. A COMPELLING GLANCE OF THE EYE, A WITTY REMARK, A SMART REJOINDER, SOME AIRY PERSIFLAGE, AND SO ONE LAUNCHES THE AFFAIR.

THIS AFTERNOON, BY ARRANGEMENT, TOOK HER FOR OUR FIRST WALK. HAD SOME DOUBTS AS REGARDS RUSHING THE AFFAIR, SHE BEING A CUT ABOVE THE AVERAGE, AS REGARDS BIRTH, BRINGING UP, ETC. HOWEVER, THE AFFAIR WENT

swimmingly.

I WAS IN GOOD VEIN, AND IN SPITE OF SOME PRELIMINARY POUTINGS SOON HAD HER QUIESCENT IN MY ARMS. WE LAY, OR RATHER HALF RECLINED, ON THE SWARD, EYES CLOSED, LIPS MURMURING, PASSION GRIPPING US BY THE THROATS. HOWEVER, I AM GLAD TO SAY THAT I HAD SUFFICIENT STRENGTH OF WILL TO LET THE AFFAIR END IN KISSES. YOU, CYNICAL OLD DEVIL THAT YOU ARE, WILL SMILE AT THIS, BUT AFTER ALL SUCH MEN AS OURSELVES ARE APT TO GET A BIT *PASSÉ* AS REGARDS THE VIRTUES. I AM NO SAINT MYSELF, AS GOD, OR RATHER THE DEVIL, KNOWS. I HAVE MADE GOOD RESOLUTIONS BEFORE, AND, I CONFESS, HAVE FAILED TO KEEP THEM. WOMEN AND DRINK HAVE EVER PLAYED THE DEVIL WITH ME AND THOUGH, LIKE YOU, I LAUGH CYNICALLY AT THE MORALITY OF PARSONS, I FRANKLY ADMIT TO YOU, WHO, LIKE MYSELF, HAVE EXPERIENCED THE FIERCE GLAMOUR OF WOMEN, THAT I'M GLAD I SPARED HER.

from *Redheap*, by Norman Lindsay, 1930

AND THE GIPSY MAN HIMSELF! YVETTE QUIVERED SUDDENLY, AS IF SHE HAD SEEN HIS BIG, BOLD EYES UPON HER, WITH THE NAKED INSINUATION OF DESIRE IN THEM. THE ABSOLUTELY NAKED INSINUATION OF DESIRE MADE HER LIE PRONE AND POWERLESS IN THE BED, AS IF A DRUG HAD CAST HER IN A NEW, ALIEN MOULD ...

'WHAT IS IT, LUCILLE,' SHE ASKED, 'THAT BRINGS PEOPLE TOGETHER? PEOPLE LIKE THE EASTWOODS, FOR INSTANCE? AND DADDY AND MAMMA, SO FRIGHTFULLY UNSUITABLE? — AND THAT GIPSY WOMAN WHO TOLD MY FORTUNE, LIKE A GREAT HORSE, AND THE GIPSY MAN, SO FINE AND DELICATELY CUT? WHAT IS IT?'

'I SUPPOSE IT'S SEX, WHATEVER THAT IS,' SAID LUCILLE.

'YES, WHAT IS IT? IT'S NOT REALLY ANYTHING *COMMON*, LIKE COMMON SENSUALITY, YOU KNOW, LUCILLE. IT REALLY ISN'T.'

'NO, I SUPPOSE NOT,' SAID LUCILLE. 'ANYHOW, I SUPPOSE IT NEEDN'T BE.'

'BECAUSE, YOU SEE, THE COMMON FELLOWS, YOU KNOW, WHO MAKE A GIRL FEEL LOW: NOBODY CARES MUCH ABOUT THEM. NOBODY FEELS ANY SORT OF CONNECTION WITH THEM. YET THEY'RE SUPPOSED TO BE THE SEXUAL SORT.'

'I SUPPOSE,' SAID LUCILLE, 'THERE'S THE LOW SORT OF SEX, AND THERE'S THE OTHER SORT, THAT ISN'T LOW. IT'S FRIGHTFULLY COMPLICATED, REALLY! I *LOATHE* COMMON FELLOWS. AND I NEVER FEEL ANYTHING *SEXUAL*' — SHE LAID A RATHER

DISGUSTED STRESS ON THE WORD — 'FOR FELLOWS WHO AREN'T COMMON.
PERHAPS I HAVEN'T GOT ANY SEX.'

'THAT'S JUST IT!' SAID YVETTE. 'PERHAPS NEITHER OF US HAS. PERHAPS WE
HAVEN'T REALLY *GOT* ANY SEX, TO *connect* US WITH MEN.'

'HOW HORRIBLE IT SOUNDS: *CONNECT US WITH MEN*!' CRIED LUCILLE, WITH
REVULSION. 'WOULDN'T YOU HATE TO BE CONNECTED WITH MEN THAT WAY?
OH, I THINK IT'S AN AWFUL PITY THERE HAS TO *BE* SEX! IT WOULD BE SO MUCH
BETTER IF WE COULD STILL BE MEN AND WOMEN, WITHOUT THAT SORT OF THING.'

from *The Virgin and the Gipsy*, by D. H. Lawrence, 1930

My dearest Girl,

This moment I have set myself to copy some verses out fair. I cannot proceed with any degree of content. I must write you a line or two and see if that will assist in dismissing you from my Mind for ever so short a time. Upon my Soul I can think of nothing else. The time is passed when I had power to advise and warn you against the unpromising morning of my Life. My love has made me selfish. I cannot exist without you. I am forgetful of everything but seeing you again — my Life seems to stop there — I see no further. You have absorb'd me. I have a sensation at the present moment as though I was dissolving — I should be exquisitely miserable without the hope of soon seeing you. I should be afraid to separate myself far from you. My sweet Fanny, will your heart never change? My love, will it? I have no limit now to my love ... Your note came in just here. I cannot be happier away from you. 'Tis richer than an Argosy of Pearles. Do not threat me even in jest. I have been astonished that Men could die Martyrs for religion — I have shudder'd at it. I shudder no more — I could be martyr'd for my Religion — Love is my religion — I could die for that. You have ravish'd me away by a Power I cannot resist; and yet I could resist till I saw you; and even since I have seen you I have endeavoured often 'to reason against the reasons of my Love.' I can do that no more — the pain would be too great.

My love is selfish. I cannot *Breathe* without you.

Yours for ever, John Keats

John Keats to Miss Fanny Brawne

Acknowledgements

The extracts from 'The Song of Solomon' from the Authorised version of the Bible (The King James Bible), the rights of which are vested in the Crown, are reproduced by permission of the Crown's patentee, Cambridge University Press.

The quotation from *Characters* by La Bruyére translated by Henri van Laun and revised by Denys C. Potts, © Oxford University Press 1963, is reproduced by permission of Oxford University Press.

The quotations from *Remembrance of Things Past* by Marcel Proust, translated by Scott Moncrieff and ·evised by Terence Martin, © Random House, Inc., and Chatto and Windus, are reprinted with the permission of the Estate of the author, the Estate of the translator, the Estate of the revisor and the publisher, Chatto and Windus.

The extract from *The Young Visiters* by Daisy Ashford is reproduced by permission of the publisher, Chatto and Windus.

The extracts from *The Virgin and The Gipsy* and *The First Lady Chatterley* by D.H. Lawrence, published by William Heinemann Ltd., are reproduced with the permission of Laurence Pollinger Ltd and the Estate of Frieda Lawrence Ravagli.

The extract from *Redheap* by Norman Lindsay, © Janet Glad, is reproduced with the permission of Angus&Robertson, a division of HarperCollins *Publishers*.

'Inner Courtyard of the Heart' by Irene Wettenhall is reproduced with the permission of the author.

'Showers' by Jeri Kroll, 'Inner Courtyard of the Heart' by Irene Wettenhall, 'Comparisons' and 'Lust and Love' by Dr. John Bray all previously appeared in *The Inner Courtyard* edited by Anne Brewster and Jeff Guess, and published by Friendly Street Poets Inc., South Australia. 'Showers' by Jeri Kroll first appeared in *Indian Movies*, published by Hyland House, 1984. 'Comparisons' by Dr. John Bray first appeared in *The Bay of Salamis and Other Poems*, published by Friendly Street Poets, 1986. 'Lust and Love' by Dr John Bray first appeared in *Poems 1972-1979*, published by ANU Press, 1979.

The extract from *Rameau's Nephew and Other Works* by Denis Diderot, © 1956 by Jacques Barzon and Ralph Bowen is used by permission of Doubleday, a division of Bantam Doubleday Dell Publishing Group, Inc.

The quotation from *Maxims* by François, duc de La Rochefoucauld, translated by Leonard Tancock (Penguin Classics, 1959) © Leonard Tancock, 1959, is reproduced by permission of Penguin Books, Ltd.

Every effort has been made to trace and acknowledge the owners of copyright material in this book. The publishers would be pleased to hear from anyone who can provide them with further information on this material.